GW00363243

IS THERE A
SEX BEFORE MARRIAGE?

Booklets taken from *Alpha: Questions of Life:*

Christianity:Boring, Untrue and Irrelevant?
Who Is Jesus?
Why Did Jesus Die?
How Can I Be Sure of My Faith?
Why and How Should I Read the Bible?
Why and How Do I Pray?
How Does God Guide Us?
The Holy Spirit
How Can I Resist Evil?
Why and How Should We Tell Others?
Does God Heal Today?
What About the Church?
How Can I Make the Most of the Rest of My Life?

Booklets taken from *Searching Issues:*

Why Does God Allow Suffering?
What About Other Religions?
Is There Anything Wrong With Sex Before Marriage?
How Does the New Age Movement Relate to Christianity?
What Is the Christian Attitude to Homosexuality?
Is There a Conflict Between Science and Christianity?
Is the Trinity Unbiblical, Unbelievable and Irrelevant?

Is There Anything Wrong with Sex Before Marriage?

NICKY GUMBEL

Alpha

First published 1994 as part of *Searching Issues,*
New edition 2002
This edition 2004

Unless otherwise indicated, biblical quotations are from the
New International Version © 1973, 1978, 1984 by the International
Bible Society. (Inclusive language version 1995, 1996.)

ISBN 1 8429 055 8

Illustrations by Charlie Mackesy

Published by
KINGSWAY COMMUNICATIONS LTD
Lottbridge Drove, Eastbourne, BN23 6NT, England.
Email: books@kingsway.co.uk

Printed in Canada.

Contents

Is There Anything Wrong with Sex Before Marriage?

A major sexual revolution took place in the second half of the twentieth century. Our society has been saturated with sexual stimulation in films, television, advertising and glossy magazines. It is not only the top shelf in newsagents which is devoted to sex; now the middle-shelf magazines tell you 'everything you wanted to know about sex, plus much much more'. Sex has become the idol of our times.

At the same time, another alarming revolution has taken place: marriage and family life is breaking down. A century ago the divorce rate was 200 per annum. By 1987 it had risen to 151,000 per annum – a three-fold increase since 1967 – and by 2002 the figure had reached 160,000 per annum. Almost one half of marriages now end in divorce. The financial cost of broken marriages, based on hard statistics such as legal aid and supplementary benefits, is a staggering £2 billion per year.[1] More importantly, the human cost is incalculable.

So we see in our society an increasing unwillingness to enter marriage in the first place. More and more couples live together without getting married. Only two in three conceptions now occur inside marriage and lead to birth. John Diamond wrote in *The Times*, 'Nowadays, for most people at least, marriage is one of those optional things you do if you want to make a particular sort of statement about the life you already share.'[2]

These changed attitudes to marriage and sex involve hidden dangers. Many people find themselves trapped in a promiscuity which destroys their self esteem, exposes them to sexually transmitted disease and often ruins their ability to form a lasting relationship. From the optimistic embrace of sexual liberation in the sixties, most people have started to see that there is something fundamentally wrong with this so called sexual liberation.

On the other hand, there have been times when the church and society have had a totally repressive and negative attitude toward sex. Origen, one of the early theologians of the church, regarded sex as something inherently sinful: 'Adam did not have sexual knowledge of his wife until after The Fall. If it had not been for The Fall, the human race would likely have been propagated in some very mysterious or angelic manner without sex and, therefore, sin.'

In the Middle Ages, Yves of Chartres taught that complete abstinence from sexual relationships had to be maintained on five out of seven days a week: on Thursdays in memory of the arrest of our Lord, on Fridays in honour of his death, on Saturdays in honour of the Virgin Mary, on Sundays in commemoration of the Resurrection, and on

Mondays out of respect for the faithful departed!

The Victorian era is also well-known for its sexual prudery when some even considered that the legs of pianos had to be covered! These prejudices and the sense of guilt associated with sex still affect the lives of many.

Both the obsession of the modern era and the repression of former times are a far cry from the biblical understanding of sex which is not outdated but highly relevant to us and our society today. Indeed, it is here that we find the Maker's instructions which bring liberation and fulfillment.

GOD, IN HIS LOVE, HAS GIVEN US A GOOD PLAN

The Bible affirms our sexuality: God made us 'male and female' (Genesis 1:27). The body is good; we are 'fearfully and wonderfully made' (Psalm 139:14). Jesus had a physical body. Everything God made was good – including our sexual organs which he designed for our enjoyment. The sexual urge is God-given and, like fire in the fireplace, is a great blessing when enjoyed in the right context. In God's original creation Adam and Eve were 'both naked, and they felt no shame' (Genesis 2:25). There was no guilt attached to their sexuality, which is why we should be able to talk openly and frankly about these matters without embarrassment. As C. S. Lewis points out, 'Pleasure is God's idea, not the Devil's.' God is not looking down from heaven and saying, 'Goodness gracious, whatever will they think of next?'

Further, the Bible celebrates sexual intimacy as a profound form of communication. 'Adam knew Eve his wife, and she conceived and bore Cain' (Genesis 4:1, RSV). In the Song of Solomon we see the delight, tenderness, contentment and satisfaction that can be derived from sexual intimacy. The tone is set in the opening verses: 'Let him kiss me with the kisses of his mouth – for your love is more delightful than wine' (Song of Songs 1:2).

Sex in its right context is good and beautiful. God has a high view of sexual relationships. Marriage is a reflection of Christ's relationship with the church (Ephesians 5) and there can be nothing higher than that. That is why Christian married couples should be encouraged to delight in one another and enjoy sexual intimacy to the full. There is great freedom within marriage and sex should never become mundane or boring. This contrasts sharply with the attitude of many so-called defenders of sexual liberation. Marcelle d'Argy Smith, editor of *Cosmopolitan*, has stated, 'Sex is like Big Ben. I'm glad it's there and if I were less tired I could go and have a look at it.'[3]

The biblical context of sexual intercourse is the lifelong commitment in marriage between one man and one woman. When Jesus spoke of marriage he went back to the creation account: 'For this reason a man will leave his father and mother and be united to his wife, and they will become one flesh' (Matthew 19:5–6 quoting Genesis 2:24).

Here we see the key to the biblical understanding of marriage. First, there is a leaving – a public act of lifelong exclusive commitment. Secondly, there is a uniting of the man and the woman. They are 'glued together' in marriage. Thirdly, it is in this context that the 'one flesh' sexual union takes place. It is not just physical and biological, but emotional, psychological, spiritual and social. Our whole beings are united in marriage, and sexual intercourse is not just a physical response to a physical desire. The physical union both expresses the other unions and also brings them about. We express ourselves with our bodies and the act of intercourse expresses our unity. 'The total physical self-giving would be a lie if it were not the sigin and fruit of a total personal self-giving . . . The only "place" in which this self-giving in its whole truth is made possible is marriage.'[4]

God has so designed our bodies and our sexuality that we can go on exploring and enjoying one another for a lifetime. An actor, well-known for his romantic roles, was asked on a TV programme, 'What makes a great lover?' He answered: 'A great lover is someone who can satisfy one woman all her life long; and who can be satisfied by one woman all his life long. A great lover is not someone who goes from woman to woman. Any dog could do that.' Of course, this applies to men and women alike.

11

Next, in God's order, partnership and procreation are linked. God blessed Adam and Eve and said to them, 'Be fruitful and increase in number' (Genesis 1:28). God so designed our bodies that the same act of intercourse should have the effect of both uniting us in partnership and being the means by which procreation takes place. This does not mean that every act of intercourse should have that intention, but it is part of God's design that it takes a man and a woman to have a baby. God's ideal is that every child should be conceived in an act that expresses love and commitment and that they should grow up in that atmosphere. The most important relationship for a child's security is the one between the two parents.

GOD, IN HIS LOVE, WARNS AGAINST HUMAN DISTORTIONS

Tragically, God's plan has been distorted by human sin. Our sin affects every area of our human lives, including our sexuality. 'All have sinned and fall short of the glory of God'

12

(Romans 3:23). Obviously, not everyone's sexuality is equally distorted, and some will retain the original creation order more than others, but none of us is in a position to pass judgement. When Jesus said to those about to stone the woman caught in adultery: 'Let anyone of you who is without sin be the first to throw a stone at her' (John 8:7), the context was not just any sin, but specifically sexual sin.

The fact that we are all guilty does not mean that it does not matter, or that we should make no attempt to avoid sin. Jesus told the woman, 'Leave your life of sin' (John 8:11). The Maker's instructions were given out of love. It is not that when he sees people enjoying themselves he says, 'I'll soon put a stop to that!' but rather that God does not want us to get hurt.

As we have seen, God designed sexual intercourse for our enjoyment in the context of marriage. Any sex outside marriage is a distortion of God's good gift and falls short of his ideal. Jesus took the Bible as his authority and if Jesus is our Lord we must follow his example. This does not mean we condemn the people involved, for we are called to accept and love people unconditionally. At the same time, we must speak out against the sin. Indeed, it is part of loving people.

Any sexual intercourse outside marriage is forbidden. Adultery is specifically outlawed by the seventh commandment, and when we see the betrayal of trust and the wreckage of families stemming from this deceit we are able to understand why. However, sex before marriage is certainly widely defended and needs more discussion.

Because sexual intercourse is a life-uniting act, Paul says that even if a man has sex with a prostitute he becomes 'one

13

with her in body' (1 Corinthians 6:16). He commands his readers to 'flee from sexual immorality' (v.18). The word he uses includes all sex outside marriage. It is the same word that Jesus used in Mark 7: 21 and Paul used elsewhere (1 Thessalonians 4:3–8).

Most would agree that sex and love should go together. Promiscuity, although common practice today, has few serious defenders, but many people would defend the practice of sex before marriage in a more stable relationship. The teaching of Jesus in the rest of the New Testament is against such a practice, for it is not just love and sex that must go together but sex and long-term commitment to each other in marriage. Such commitment is evidenced in our society by the marriage vows. Marriage is not just a piece of paper, nor is the wedding day simply for dressing-up and getting together with family and friends. It is a public and responsible expression of lifelong commitment, and the certificate of marriage is a public document accessible to all. In this context, sexual intercourse signifies, seals and brings about an unbreakable, total personal unity. Without such a commitment, sex is cheapened, being 'a life-uniting act without a life-uniting intent'.[5] The life-uniting intent is evidenced by marriage alone; engagement is not sufficient, for engagements can always be broken (this is part of the point of a period of engagement). Irrevocable commitment comes only with the public act of marriage.

This is God's pattern for sexual relationships. Sex outside marriage may feel good. However, when God's pattern is broken people get hurt.

First, we risk hurting ourselves. When a relationship

involving sexual intercourse breaks down, one or both parties get hurt. This is true both in the case of divorce and in sexual relationships between unmarried people. Pre-marital sex increases the chances of extra-marital sex and, of course, adultery is one of the leading factors in marriage breakdown. Marriage is far more likely to work if the couple have not lived together. Recent figures have indicated that the divorce rate is far lower among those who have waited until their wedding day. For example, according to recent research of couples who married for the first time in the 1980s, those who lived together before marriage were 60 per cent more likely to have divorced after eight years of marriage than similar couples who had not done so.[6]

If we keep to God's laws, we live under his blessing, and part of that blessing will be the blessing of the wedding day. Even those who are not Christians often recognise that they have lost something by living together before the marriage. John Diamond, writing in *The Times* about those who have waited until their wedding day, says they

> have something to look forward to. They leave their parents' home on the morning of the wedding as children and climb into bed that night as adults. There is so much to play with, and all at the same time: the new house, the giggling joint washing-up sessions, the bed, the joint cheque book – and because it all started with the wedding, it all becomes part of the same adventure.
>
> The rest of us, the over-the-broomstick lot, get up, tap our partners on the shoulder, make jokey gulping noises, get a mini-cab round to the register office, listen to our mates making faux-ironic jokes about what we will be getting up to

tonight, ho-ho, and then come back and do last night's washing-up. We try out the new Mr and Mrs names for a day or two, then realize that our joint cheque book and the mortgage deeds are in the old names anyway, and go back to them.

We've done check books a dozen times and deciding on the new paint for the hall a hundred. There is nothing new you can tell us about the socks-on-the-bathroom-floor conundrum; and whose-turn-is-it-for-Waitrose mantra is one that we already know by heart. While newly met newlyweds can set sail on their magical voyage of discovery, our own marital plans mean we are stuck on the Woolwich ferry arguing about who forgot to bring the packed lunch.[7]

If two people who are already involved in a sexual relationship do eventually marry each other, they often regret that they did not wait until their wedding day.

The Revd Gordon Harman recalls from his childhood that he and his brother once came across an old black trunk whilst playing in a storeroom at their home. When they took the lid off, they discovered to their delight a complete model railway. They loved it, and felt sure it would be theirs one day. As each Christmas came and went, they experienced first disappointment and then guilt. Finally, the real day came and they put on a pretence of surprise, but both knew that they had partly ruined the gift.

When we embark on a sexual relationship at the wrong time we often induce patterns of guilt and frustration and run the risk of tainting the gift of our sexuality. People often say that they have sensed an indefinable purity and beauty at a wedding where both the husband and wife have waited for each other. One couple I know who did sleep together before marriage say that one of their greatest regrets is not to have experienced that God-given blessing on their own wedding day.

Secondly, we risk hurting others. If a sexual relationship does not last, it may have a damaging effect on a future marriage. Previous sexual relationships can lead to jealousy and resentment for the uniqueness of the sexual act has been compromised. It can be particularly difficult when a husband or wife comes into contact with a previous partner.

Sexual relationships before marriage can make marriage itself less likely. Although our society apparently accepts the idea of a string of sexual relationships, there are not many people who set out to marry someone with a long and complex sexual past. The hurt involved can be very serious. If there is an unwanted pregnancy, then hard decisions have to be made.

Thirdly, we risk hurting society. The family unit is one of the basic building blocks of society. Increasingly, it is recognised that sex outside marriage can be a factor that leads to family breakdown. In turn, family breakdown is one of the reasons for the soaring crime rate. In fact, both are symptoms of a society which has turned away from God's standards. Immanuel Jakobovits, Chief Rabbi from 1967–1991, writing about marital infidelity, said that 'the cost to society is incalculable: above all in terms of the millions of children now being raised in a moral wasteland, without the shelter of a loving home. Is it any wonder that from their number, countless embittered, selfish, lonely and sometimes violent citizens are recruited to swell the ranks of the anti-social?'[8]

Before AIDS promiscuity was unhealthy; now it can be fatal. For too long the glossy magazines fooled us that 'free love' was free. But there is a price to be paid. If we had kept to God's standards, AIDS would not have spread. The best way to stop it now is to return to God's standards.

Fourthly, we hurt God. The most important consideration of all is that breaking God's laws has serious consequences: it cuts us off from him. That is why it is impossible to hold together a wholehearted love and service of God and disobedience in the area of sexual morality. It is this which stops many today giving their lives to Christ, and they lose out on abundant and eternal life for something which in the long run only does them harm. Others are torn apart by the tension in their lives between a supposed profession of faith and a life which they know goes against such a profession.

The New Testament warns us that God will judge all sin, including immorality (1 Thessalonians 4:6). God's laws are there to protect us and to protect society – given out of love. But there are serious consequences when we break his laws.

GOD, IN HIS LOVE, SENT JESUS TO RESTORE US

God's standards are very high and in our society they are not easy to keep. However, God has not left us alone and he came to set us free. He did not come to condemn the world but to save it, giving us the power to resist temptation, and to bring forgiveness and healing.

How to resist
It is possible to stop having sexual intercourse, even though

18

it may be very difficult. When someone comes to Christ, they may be in a sexual relationship with a partner who is not a Christian. It may be hard to explain to that person why they will not sleep with them any more, and it could result in feelings of rejection and hurt. Yet it is almost impossible to make any real progress in the Christian faith until such a sexual relationship ends, because we cannot hold on to sin and be wholehearted in our Christian lives at the same time. If both parties come to Christ at the same time, it is easier, but it still requires great self-control. I have seen several couples who have succeeded in this area and have found enrichment from God in their relationship. Usually they have married later and found God's blessing also in their family life. Some think they will lose the respect of their friends, but the opposite is often the case. If we live by these standards, we will have an opportunity to influence society, rather than being squeezed into the world's mould.

Many fear that there will be a gap in their lives if they stop making love, and that they will not be as close to their partner. This is not the case unless sex is the sole basis for the relationship, in which case it is better that the relationship ends because it lacks a solid foundation. Indeed, this is one of the dangers of sex before marriage: it clouds our judgement about the rightness of the relationship. It is much easier to work out whether we are suited to be partners for life if our judgement is unclouded by a sexual relationship. As one twenty-seven-year-old woman put it: 'Once the sex had been taken away, I realized there was nothing left.' If the relationship is right, there will not be such a gap; rather there will be a depth of understanding, respect, trust and dignity.

19

There may even be a sense of relief. Another woman said, 'I felt as though a huge weight, which I hadn't realised was there, lifted off my shoulders.' Sexual intercourse is not the only way to demonstrate love. In fact, self-control often shows more love and sets a good pattern for married life when, from time to time, self-control needs to be exercised. If the relationship is conducted along these lines, it makes it easier for both parties to decide whether or not it is right to get married.

How do we avoid getting into such a situation in the first place? Jesus began with the heart, the eyes and the thoughts. He said, 'Anyone who looks at a woman lustfully has already committed adultery with her in his heart' (Matthew 5:28). This is where self-control begins for us all. All of us will be tempted to have immoral thoughts – Jesus was tempted also – but temptation is not sin. It is not the thoughts that are sinful; rather it is the entertaining of them. The more we give in, the more difficult it gets. The more we resist, the easier it gets. James, the brother of Jesus, wrote, 'Resist the devil, and he will flee from you. Come near to God and he will come near to you' (James 4:7–8). It tends to be a spiral, either going up or down.

We need to help one another by not putting temptation in the way. For example, it is not a good idea to sleep in the same bed if you are trying to resist temptation. Single people sometimes ask, 'How far can we go?' The Bible does not lay down the rules and nor should we. People and circumstances vary. We need to remember that it is always hard not to go further next time. It is also worth considering how you would feel if the relationship did end. It is much

20

easier to maintain respect, dignity and friendship if you have exercised restraint in this area.

If the relationship continues to marriage, nothing is lost. In fact, the reverse is true. No married couple I know ever regretted going too slowly before they were married.

If all this leads then to great sexual frustration, is masturbation a way out? This can be a taboo subject, especially among Christian people. In fact, nearly all adolescents and many adults do masturbate. It is estimated that 95 percent of men and over 50 percent of women have some experience of masturbation. Of course, it is not physically harmful and it is nowhere specifically condemned in the Bible.

However, there are three concerns. First, it has a tendency to become obsessive. Secondly, it depersonalizes sex – our sexuality was intended to move us toward personal communion. Thirdly, it is often associated with lustful thoughts. But the guilt that usually accompanies masturbation is out of all proportion to its seriousness. Martin Luther describes it as 'a puppy sin'. One pastor said it was like 'biting our nails' – something many do as part of growing up. It is not a good idea, but should not be taken too seriously unless it becomes excessive.

In all these areas we need to avoid the guilt and condemnation spiral which can bring us down and lead us to further sin. The Spirit of God sets us free where a set of rules would be powerless (Romans 8:1–4). Jesus' provision of the Holy Spirit means that it is possible to break free.

Forgiveness

As we have seen earlier, all of us have failed in this area to a greater or lesser extent. None of us is in a position to throw stones at anyone else. Jesus died for us so that we could be forgiven. The way to receive forgiveness is through repentance. In Psalm 51 we see a model for repentance following sexual sin. This is the psalm attributed to David after he had committed adultery with Bathsheba. The remedy for sin is not to make excuses or to do things to make up for it. Rather it is confession and repentance. However far we have fallen, we can make a new start in Christ.

I love the story Jackie Pullinger tells of a seventy-two-year-old woman in her church who was a heroin addict and a prostitute for sixty years. She used to sit outside a brothel waiting for customers, poking the sewers with a stick so that they would flow more freely. She was being injected in her back three times a day because there were no more veins in her arms and legs. She had no identity card and did not even exist as far as the Hong Kong government was concerned. She was 'one of those who are not'. Seven years ago she gave her life to Jesus Christ and received forgiveness for her sins. She went to live in one of Jackie's houses and God started to heal her. In the summer of 1992, she married Little Wa who was aged seventy-five. Jackie described it as 'the wedding of the decade'. The former prostitute was able to walk down the aisle in white, cleansed and forgiven by Jesus Christ.

Jesus enables us both to receive forgiveness and to give it. Many have been sinned against in this area. Some say that one person in ten has been sexually abused, and often people go through life crippled by these experiences. Freedom always begins with forgiveness – receiving God's forgiveness and then, in gratitude for his forgiveness, forgiving those who have sinned against us.

CONCLUSION

The heart of our sexuality is not the biological dimension but the personal one. Jesus himself points the way to a state beyond marriage. In heaven there will be no marriage. Here on this earth, as John Stott, himself unmarried, writes,

> it is possible for human sexual energy to be redirected ('sublimated' would be the Freudian word) both into affectionate relationships with friends of both sexes and into the loving service of others. Multitudes of Christian singles, both men and women, can testify to this. Alongside a natural loneliness, accompanied sometimes by acute pain, we can find joyful self-fulfillment in the self-giving service of God and other people.[9]

Sex is not an ultimate goal. Our society, as we have seen at the beginning, has made an idol out of sex. Sex has replaced God as the object of worship. We need to reverse this. If we seek pleasure as a god, in the long run we find emptiness, disappointment and addiction. If we seek God, we find, among other things, ecstatic pleasure.

23

FOR FURTHER READING

Lewis Smedes, *Sex for Christians* (Triangle SPCK, 1993).
Richard Foster, *Money, Sex and Power* (Hodder & Stoughton, 1985).
John White, *Eros Defiled* (IVP, 1977).

NOTES

1. Statistics from *The Times* (31st May 1989).
2. *The Times* (21st May 1992).
3. *Daily Mail* (9th February 1993).
4. Pope John Paul II, *Familiaris Consortio: Theology of the Body* (The Vatican, 1981), p11.
4. Lewis Smedes, *Sex for Christians* (Triangle, SPCK, 1993), p130.
5. John Haskey. Pre-marital cohabitation and the probability of divorce: analyses using new data from the General Household Survey. *Population Trends 68* (HMSO Publications), quoted in *The Times* (19th June 1992).
6. *The Times* (25th June 1992).
7. *The Times* (22nd September 1993).
8. John Stott, *The Message of the Thessalonians* (IVP, 1991), pp84–85.

The Alpha Course

The Alpha course is a practical introduction to the Christian faith initiated by Holy Trinity Brompton in London, and now being run by thousands of churches, of many denominations, throughout the world.

For more information on the Alpha course, and details of tapes, videos and training manuals, contact the Publications office, on 0845 644 7544 or visit our website at alphacourse.org

To order any course materials call
The Alpha Publications Hotline:

To order from overseas:
Tel +44 1228 611749
Fax +44 1228 514949

Alpha

Alpha titles available

Why Jesus?   A booklet given to all participants at the start of the Alpha course. 'The clearest, best illustrated and most challenging short presentation of Jesus that I know." – Michael Green

Why Christmas?   The Christmas version of *Why Jesus?*

Alpha: Questions of Life   The Alpha course in book form. In fifteen compelling chapters Nicky Gumbel points the way to an authentic Christianity which is exciting and relevant to today's world.

A Life Worth Living   What happens after Alpha? Based on the book of Philippians, this is an invaluable next step for those who have just completed the Alpha course, and for anyone eager to put their faith on a firm biblical footing.

How to Run the Alpha Course: Telling Others   The theological principles and the practical details of how courses are run. Each alternate chapter consists of a testimony of someone whose life has been changed by God through an Alpha course.

Challenging Lifestyle   Studies in the Sermon on the Mount showing how Jesus' teaching flies in the face of modern lifestyle and presents us with a radical alternative.

30 Days   Nicky Gumbel selects thirty passages from the Old and New Testament which can be read over thirty days. It is designed for those on an Alpha course and others who are interested in beginning to explore the Bible.

The Heart of Revival   Ten Bible studies based on the book of Isaiah, drawing out important truths for today by interpreting some of the teaching of the Old Testament prophet Isaiah. The book seeks to understand what revival might mean and how we can prepare to be part of it.

All titles are by Nicky Gumbel, who is on the staff of
Holy Trinity Brompton